thank you
friend

a collection of poems,
prayers, stories, quotes, and
scriptures to say thank you

HOWARD
®PUBLISHING CO.

thank you friend

thank you friend

thank you friend

thank you friend

thank you friend tha

thank you friend thank you friend thank you friend thank you friend

friend

thank you

Talking excitedly

both at once

or sitting in

comfortable

silence, our

hearts always

hear.

thank
you

friend

Dear *Faith*,

God gave me a matchless gift when He gave me you. The most wonderful miracle is that someone whom I respect, admire, and love—you—could feel the same way toward me.

Thank you for touching my life in ways both ordinary and extraordinary. Many of my most pleasant memories and hopes and dreams for the future include you. I like that you know so much about me—my darkest secrets, my most private yearnings, my failings and triumphs. Your trustworthy and loving nature makes it easy for me to be myself, to feel understood and valued, never vulnerable.

Thank you for being a reliable yet kind mirror, not letting me get away with hiding from or covering the truth about myself, but still seeing me in the best possible light. As you have loved me, you have enabled me to love myself, and I hope I can return that blessing to you. Thank you for being my friend.

With deep gratitude and love,

We do not wish
for friends to feed
and clothe our
bodies—neighbors
are kind enough
for that—but to do
the like office for
our spirits.

HENRY DAVID THOREAU

A genuine friendship
is a heavenly present.
It blesses our hearts
because God's love is in it.

—Evelyn McCurdy

Dedication

Y ou're the most dedicated person I know," Leah said, both admiration and disapproval in her tone. She tossed a pillow at her friend Brandi, who dozed on the porch lounge chair surrounded by Chaucer, Shakespeare, and a collection of American authors. Brandi awoke with a start, sending Shakespeare crashing to the floor unceremoniously.

"Oh, Leah, it's you." Brandi let out her breath as an awareness of time and place flooded back. "I must have just dozed off," she said, willing it to be so. "Oh no!" she gasped with horror as she looked at her watch. "I've slept for nearly two hours. I've missed American lit!" She jumped up and scrambled to gather her books and papers.

"Relax," Leah commanded. "It's too late to make that class," she reasoned, "and it won't hurt you to miss one. That's what college students do occasionally—skip class." Brandi sagged back onto the chair in resignation.

"Besides," Leah continued, "the sleep will do you more good than any review of James and Hawthorne. You're trying to do too much," Leah said with conviction. "You're exhausted. You can't work full-time, go to school full-time, and take care of a husband and kids too. Something's got to give, and I hope it's not your health or your sanity."

"I know," Brandi acknowledged wearily, putting her head back and closing her eyes, "but I can't stop any of it. I love my job—it's challenging and fulfilling—but they made an exception when they promoted me. The position requires a degree. I feel like I've got to finish school before the bubble bursts and someone decides I'm not really qualified."

"You're a great communications officer," Leah protested.

"Without a degree in communications," Brandi countered.

"You worked your way up with outstanding performance," Leah defended her friend. "That says a lot about your ability."

"Yes," Brandi chuckled, grateful for her friend's confidence. "Now all I need is a degree to go with it."

She followed Leah into the house. Leah paused to empty

Dedication

her pockets and change purse into the oversized Coke bottle bank that stood in a nook by the fireplace.

"Wow, it's really getting full," Brandi said, impressed. "Have you decided what you're going to do with it this time?"

"I've got some ideas," Leah said as she went to the kitchen.

Ever since Brandi had known her, Leah had collected her spare change. The bank easily held a few hundred dollars, and when it was full, she'd buy herself something special.

Leah poured them each some raspberry tea. "If I were you, I'd spend it on a vacation," Brandi advised. "Just get away from everything for a while."

"Spoken like a tired woman," Leah sympathized.

"I don't know what's wrong with me lately," Brandi admitted, rubbing her tight neck muscles. "It seems to get harder and harder to juggle everything. It didn't used to be this tough."

"It's piling up on you," Leah told her. "No one can keep up that pace for long."

"I'm going to have to," Brandi said resolutely. "At least until the semester break." She finished her tea and sighed wearily. "I have to get home and figure out what to make for dinner."

"Oh, no, you don't," Leah said mischievously. "I called Bill and told him not to wait up for you tonight. He's going to get dinner for the kids. Tomorrow's Saturday—no work or school. We're going to have a girls' night out."

"But my studying...," Brandi protested weakly, but her eyes shone with anticipation and appreciation. Leah was a wonderful friend who watched out for her. It was Leah who had encouraged Brandi to stop by—Leah's house was conveniently located between campus and work—to study or rest whenever she could grab a few moments away. It was Leah who brought dinner for Brandi and her family once a week. Brandi knew she hadn't had nearly enough time for her friend since starting school, but Leah never complained. She simply pitched in however she could to lighten Brandi's heavy load. Whatever Leah had planned for her tonight, Brandi could hardly wait.

They spent the night in a time warp that took Brandi back twenty years to a childhood she could scarcely remember and that she was sure had never been so pleasant. The stress and weariness receded with the years.

The clear October night was crisp and cool. The smell of leaves and the distinctive scent of autumn air were delightful as they sat on lawn chairs in Leah's backyard.

Dedication

They toasted marshmallows over the gas grill, made s'mores, and guzzled milk like two kids. They admired the harvest moon and stars on a velvet-black sky, serenaded by the sleepy music of crickets. They talked and laughed about everything and nothing.

"You really do need a break," Leah said softly when they had been silent awhile. "Can't you drop a class or take a semester off?"

"If I do, I'll lose my scholarship," Brandi confided. "I can't afford that. But you know," she continued earnestly, "even though it wears me out, I feel somehow more empowered and alive than I ever have. College has opened my eyes to a whole new world of possibilities. I've discovered that I love literature."

She paused, and when she continued, her voice was low and conspiratorial. "I've never admitted this to anyone else," she told Leah. "Bill and my family would laugh at me if I told them."

"What?" Leah pressed, interested.

"My classes have awakened something else in me. My professors say I'm pretty good, but I know the odds are against me..."

"What?" Leah asked again, impatiently.

"I want to be a writer." She practically whispered it, then held her breath and waited for Leah's reaction.

After a pause, Leah spoke: "I suppose it's difficult to get published," she started slowly, "but if you approach writing with the same dedication you do everything else, I have no doubt you'll be an outstanding writer."

Brandi was pleased with her friend's response to her fragile dream. "Of course, I have such trouble finding a quiet spot and time to write," she said with a laugh, "when I finally do, I may discover I'm an awful writer after all."

The two friends laughed, then grew quiet with their thoughts. The chill in the air made them both shiver, and they reluctantly realized they would have to go inside soon.

"Maybe when you and Bill go to the cabin next weekend you can find a few hours of solitude to write," Leah suggested.

"We're going to have to cancel," Brandi said wistfully.

"Not your getaway!" Leah protested. "That's your special tradition every year."

Brandi shrugged. "Bill can't take time away from his business right now. I considered going alone...what I wouldn't give for a few days all to myself...But with my tuition and Robbie's braces, it's probably better not to have that expense," she said bravely. "Bill's mother is still coming to take care of the kids. It's

Dedication

too late to change her ticket, so maybe I'll get a little time to write. But I'll miss that beautiful mountain view..."

Leah insisted that Brandi spend the night in her guest room. She provided everything Brandi needed or wanted, and Brandi felt like a pampered princess as she fell asleep in the huge, beautiful canopy bed surrounded by pillows.

She slept more soundly than she had in weeks and was awakened at ten o'clock the next morning when Leah brought her a delicious breakfast in bed.

"Leah, this has been simply wonderful," Brandi said, her voice cracking with emotion and gratitude. "I feel relaxed and refreshed." She hugged her friend tightly. "Thank you for everything. You can't know how much this has meant to me."

Brandi drove the fifteen miles home with a smile on her face as she thought about how blessed she was to have such a friend. How restored she felt with just a little break from the stress when her soul was nurtured and fed.

It took her a while to be conscious of a strange clinking coming from the back of the car. She heard it every time she turned a corner or went over a bump. Was something wrong with the car? *That's all we need,* Brandi thought.

She pulled over and went to the rear of the car to search for the source of the noise. Everything seemed OK. *Maybe something's rolling around in the trunk,* she thought.

When she opened it, her mouth dropped open in disbelief. The entire trunk was covered with coins. She knew right away they were from Leah's bank, but the note explained it all.

Brandi,

I can't think of anything more special to do with this money than to invest it. Go by yourself to the cabin. Relax, rest, and write. I know you can do it! Dedicate the first book you publish to me, will you?

Love,

Leah

Brandi could barely see through the tears to drive. The money for the getaway was a wonderful, loving gift. But even better than that was the validation and support expressed in the note. Brandi knew she was the luckiest woman alive.

Dedication

thank you friend

thank you friend

thank you friend

thank you friend thank

thank you friend

thank you friend thank you friend thank you friend thank you friend thank you friend

friend

thank
you

Faith has power.

Your belief in

me has changed

my life.

a blessing
for you

May patience and forgiveness

Mark your friendships day by day.

May your heart be ever open

To God's touch along your way.

friend

When your soul is tired and weary,

Some of my strength I will lend.

May you always know that my love

Is the love of a faithful friend.

Of all the means
to ensure happiness
throughout the
whole of life,
by far the most
important is the
acquisition of
friends.

EPICURUS

thank you friend
thank you
thank you friend
thank you friend
thank you

thank you friend thank you friend tha

thank you friend thank you friend thank you friend thank you friend

friend

thank
you

Thank you for

knowing exactly

what I need...and

taking me out for

ice cream anyway.

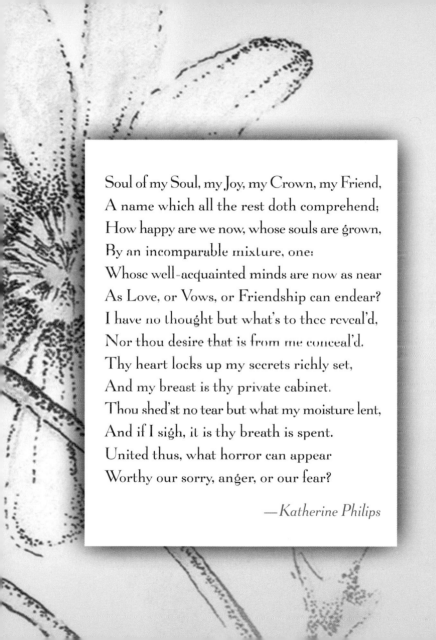

Soul of my Soul, my Joy, my Crown, my Friend,
A name which all the rest doth comprehend;
How happy are we now, whose souls are grown,
By an incomparable mixture, one:
Whose well-acquainted minds are now as near
As Love, or Vows, or Friendship can endear?
I have no thought but what's to thee reveal'd,
Nor thou desire that is from me conceal'd.
Thy heart locks up my secrets richly set,
And my breast is thy private cabinet.
Thou shed'st no tear but what my moisture lent,
And if I sigh, it is thy breath is spent.
United thus, what horror can appear
Worthy our sorry, anger, or our fear?

—Katherine Philips

thank
you

Silences make the real conversations between friends. Not the saying, but the never needing to say is what counts.

MARGARET LEE RUNBECK

Maid of Honor

 And the groom was sweating so profusely that when he picked up the ring and tried to put it on Melissa's finger, it squirted out of his fingers, hit the floor, and rolled under the organ!" Samantha recounted the day's events into the cell phone, laughing so hard she was in tears.

"You're kidding!" her best friend, Maggie, eight hundred miles away, squealed into the phone in mock horror and sheer delight.

"Scott looked horrified," Samantha continued. "Melissa started to cry—but I'm not sure if that was because of the ring or because she was hurt when the ring bearer practically knocked her down as he scrambled after the ring."

"Oh, no," Maggie interjected. "What happened then?"

"I caught her!" Samantha crowed proudly. "Like any maid of

honor would do. Like I've always done for my little sister. My flowers got a little crushed, but better the bouquet than the bride."

"Yeah, Sammy!" Maggie exulted. "Did they get the ring?"

"Not until after the ceremony," Samantha explained. "You'll love this part—I loaned them the friendship ring you gave me as a substitute during the ceremony. So in a way, you got to be part of the wedding after all."

Already feeling emotional, that was all it took to make Maggie break into tears. "I'm glad," she whispered. "Thanks for making me a part of things and telling me all the details."

"I wish I could be there with you," Sam said, sobered by her friend's tears.

"No, I wish I could be there with you," Maggie corrected. "I'm sorry I had to miss this special day."

"It's not your fault, Mag," Samantha consoled her. "What are the odds that you'd unexpectedly have to undergo surgery the morning after a wedding that's been planned for months?"

"I know." Maggie was crying again. She tried to be silent, but she knew Samantha was hard to fool.

"I'm so sorry, Mag. She's my only sister. I'm her maid of

Maid of Honor

honor. She's dreamed of this since she was a little girl. I just couldn't back out at the last minute."

Maggie knew Sam was trying to convince herself more than her friend, and she understood perfectly. It still didn't make it easy to have her best friend—the person best able to calm and encourage her—far away as she faced exploratory surgery.

"It's OK, Sam," Maggie tried to sound brave. "I know you'd be here if you could. It's not your fault I'm so far away. If David had waited, I'm sure a promotion would have opened up at the home office. Then we'd still be just down the street from you, not halfway across the country where we don't know anyone."

Now Maggie was really feeling sorry for herself, and she could no longer weep silently. She could feel Samantha's discomfort even over the increasingly bad connection of the cell phone and the crowd sounds in the background.

"What...," Samantha said. Maggie could tell she was speaking to someone else. "Look, I'm awfully sorry to have to do this," Samantha apologized to Maggie, "but I've got to go. The bride and groom hope to get all the pictures taken and make a short appearance at the reception before their 9:30 flight."

"Promise me you'll call me in the morning before my surgery?" Maggie asked anxiously before Samantha could hang up. "It's scheduled for 8:30. I go into the hospital to be prepped at 6:00."

"I promise," Samantha said solemnly. "On my honor as a friend—and as a maid of honor," she finished, trying to lighten things up a bit. "Keep your cell phone with you as long as possible."

"I will," Maggie agreed.

"I love you, Mag," Samantha told her. "And I'm praying for you. Everything's going to turn out OK."

And then she was gone, leaving Maggie with conflicting feelings of joy for having talked to her friend, gratitude for Sam's friendship, disappointment that Sam couldn't be with her, and fear about the surgery. She knew she was making too big of a deal about it. It was just outpatient surgery. And the doctor had assured her the odds were good that the shadow on her mammogram would be a benign cyst.

But Maggie couldn't get past her family history. As a teen she had watched her mother die of breast cancer. Samantha had been there and understood Maggie's fears as no one else could. That's why it felt unbearable to face tomorrow without her.

Maid of Honor

"What time is it now?" Maggie asked her husband for the hundredth time as they waited in the hospital room.

"It's 7:30," David said, trying to be patient. "I wish you'd fought as hard to keep your watch as you did that cell phone," he teased. "Then you could track the time for yourself."

"She's going to call," Maggie said, staring at the phone, willing it to ring.

"She'd better hurry," Dave said softly.

Just then, the phone rang. Maggie jumped, startled, then pounced on the phone. "Samantha?" she said hopefully.

"Maggie!" came Samantha's reassuring voice.

"Samantha, I can hardly hear you," Maggie said, panic edging her voice. "There's so much noise here..." She motioned frantically for Dave to shut the door of her room. "And the connection is bad," she said with growing despair.

"Can't... you...bad...fading...try..." was all Maggie could hear.

"Sam, don't go!" she spoke loudly. "I need to talk to you!"

"Go away!" she shouted to whoever was knocking on her door. She simply wouldn't let the nurses wheel her to surgery before she had told Samantha how much she meant to her—just in case.

"Sam? Sam!" Maggie shouted into the phone more desperately as she saw Dave move toward the door to open it.

It was all happening too fast. It wasn't supposed to happen like this!

"Yes?" came Samantha's voice, but it wasn't the distant, broken-up sound of her cell phone. It was clear and comforting, like her best friend was right there in the room with her.

"Eeeeee!" Maggie squealed in surprise and utter delight as she looked up to see Samantha standing in the door. Sam was still wearing her peach-colored maid-of-honor dress. She raced to Maggie's bedside and embraced her friend. Both friends were crying, but these were tears of joy.

"How could you...you must have driven all night!" she said accusingly, yet admiringly, to Sam.

"Yep." Sam smiled at Maggie. "I left just as the bride and groom pulled away. Didn't have time to change or stop for flowers." She extended a slightly smashed bouquet to Maggie. "Will this do?"

"Oh yes," Maggie whispered, overcome with emotion. "They're perfect. Everything is just perfect. Thank you!"

Maid of Honor

thank you friend

thank you friend

thank you friend thank

thank you friend

thank you

thank you friend

thank you friend thank you friend thank you friend thank you friend

friend

thank
you

Whether my

heart whispers,

whimpers, or

shouts; your

heart hears,

understands,

and embraces.

thank
you

The road to a friend's house is never long.

DANISH PROVERB

There are those who pass like ships in the night.
Who meet for a moment, then sail out of sight
With never a backward glance of regret;
Folks we know briefly then quickly forget.
Then there are friends who sail together
Through quiet waters and stormy weather
Helping each other through joy and through strife.
And they are the kind who give meaning to life.

—*Anonymous*

thank you friend thank you friend thank you friend thank you friend tha...

thank you friend thank you friend thank you friend thank you friend thank you friend

friend

thank
you

Your friendship

is like fresh rain

on the garden of

my soul.

thank
you

friend

Dear Heavenly Father,

I'm humbled and honored that You entrusted to me this wonderful friend. What a delight she has been through the years; what an encourager, comforter, inspiration, and anchor for my soul. Everything I could need or want in a friend, You have provided in her.

Lord, help me never to take our friendship for granted. Nurture and bless our relationship as we strive always to treat each other with the respect and care necessary for friends and friendships to thrive. May she never doubt Your love for her— or mine. May she always feel appreciated, valued, loved, and embraced.

As she has blessed me and fulfilled so many needs and desires in such a loving and generous manner, so now bless her and give her the desires of her heart.

Amen.

A FRIEND LOVES AT ALL TIMES.

Proverbs 17:17

NIV